W9-DJQ-256

High Gear

From Motorcycles to Superwheels

Written by C. J. Naden

Troll Associates

Library of Congress Catalog Card Number: 79-64637
ISBN 0-89375-248-7   (0-89375-262-2 soft cover ed.)

*Photo credits: Mary Grothe, Cycle Guide, Dan Rubin, Motobecane
America, Dave Friedman Photography, Seth Dorfler*

Everybody's on wheels! Big wheels, little wheels, fast wheels and slow. If you like explosive drag-strip action, or the solid throb of a big street bike, there is a cycle for you. If you aim to chew up the Salt Flats in a speed record try, or take a slow spin out to the lake, there is a cycle for you too. C'mon—everybody's on wheels!

The Motorized Pedal Bike—most people call it a "moped." It may not be much for speed, but it's great fun to ride. The top speed of a moped is about 40 kilometers an hour (25 miles an hour). Mopeds are not fast enough to be legal on the highway.

...to take you where you want to go.

Even though it isn't a road burner, a moped will get you where
you want to go. And you can go for long distances on the mixture
of gas and oil that is burned in the small two-stroke engine.
Although these little machines look very modern, they have
been around since the early part of this century.

There's always room to park a moped.

Mopeds were first used in Europe, where many people ride bikes and where much of the land is hilly. These motorized bikes do not have starters. You must start the engine by pedaling, in the same way you pedal a bicycle. But chugging up a hill, or spinning out to the courts, mopeds are lots of fun.

The smart thing to wear.

Mopeds cannot be ridden on highways. Therefore, in most states it is not necessary to have a license. But some states do require licenses and insurance and safety helmets. Even if it is not required, a safety helmet is the smart thing to wear.

A powerful, colorful street bike.

A step up to faster action is the street bike. Licenses and helmets are a must here. Street bikes are the most popular of all motorcycles, the kind you see on streets and highways. There are about 100 different models of street bikes, and many different engine sizes, from 100 cc (cubic centimeters) to 1,200 cc. For beginners, up to 200 cc are best.

A great transportation machine.

A motorcycle that is built for street riding must have good brakes and lights. It must have dual mirrors, directional signals, and side reflectors. Most street bikes are used for transportation. They travel on the same streets as automobile traffic. So it takes some practice to ride them safely.

Easy riding…

It may take practice to become a good street-bike rider, but it is not hard to learn how. Your right hand operates the lever for the front brake. Your left hand works the clutch. Your right foot operates the rear brake, and your left foot operates the shift. Your right hand rotates the right twistgrip for the gas.

...and a safe rider.

Day or night, street-bike riders keep their headlights on for safety. They also wear protective safety helmets. Many riders wear protective leather clothing and gloves. A few safety rules help keep much of the danger out of motorcycling.

Street bikes are used in all kinds of weather.

Street bikes are popular because they can go just about anywhere on very little fuel, and park just about anyplace. When you are sitting on a bike that is stopped, you should be able to touch the ground with both feet. If you can't, the bike is too big for you. A bike that is too big means you do not have control. And that means "trouble ahead."

Some street bikes are "official." Government messengers—or "couriers"—often carry important documents in pouches strapped to their bikes. They can get from one place to another with as little delay as possible. This messenger service is fast, convenient, and thrifty, too.

The endurance winner.

Some motorcycles are "touring bikes." To prove the toughness of cycle and rider, a Marine rode a touring bike from coast to coast across the United States. At one point, he rode for 24 hours without stopping, except to refuel. The only "extra" added to the bike was a larger-than-normal gas tank.

On the Superbike speedway.

Meet the "cream" of the street-bike class—the Superbike. You
can buy these bikes from any dealer. With some changes made
to the exhaust system, the street bike turns into a Superbike.
Instead of spinning down the highway, they zoom around the
racetrack.

At the starting line.

To race a Superbike, you must be a professional rider. Superbike events are called Production races. Six Production races
are held each year across the United States. They are known
as the National Championship Series.

Out in front.

The National Championship Series starts in March and ends in the fall. Each race is 80 kilometers (50 miles) long. Races are held at race circuits in California, New Hampshire, and Pennsylvania, and at the Daytona International Speedway in Florida.

Coming out of a turn and into the straightaway.

As in many motorcycle and auto road races, riders fight for the fastest time around the twisting road-race circuits. But unlike most other races, there are no pit stops in a Production race. The riders cannot refuel. Smart riders know how to handle the Superbike for the most distance on the least fuel. But if you run out of gas, it's all over. You're out of the race!

Plenty of crowding at the turns.

A Production race is noisy and exciting, especially when the riders bunch together at the turns. Superbikes reach very high speeds. But they go a lot slower at the turns. In a race, the headlights of these cycles are covered with tape. The tape protects riders from flying glass, in case of an accident.

Safe riding counts, too.

With big, powerful machines at high speeds, there is always danger on the track. The riders wear safety helmets and goggles or face shields to protect themselves in case of a spill. They also wear boots, gloves, and leather clothing called "leathers."

...he "parade lap."

Some street bikes have sidecars. A race official in a sidecar leads
the Superbikes once around the track before the action begins.
This is called a "parade lap." It gives the fans a good look at the
riders. Sometimes bikes with sidecars have events of their own.
They are called "Elephant Rallies."

A "full-dress" touring bike can carry a lot.

Professional riders come from all parts of the country to enter Production races. Both men and women riders are part of the pro circuit. Some fans arrive on fancy touring bikes, loaded with all their luggage.

On the drag strip.

Superbikes are big, fast, and noisy. But they can't match the monsters of the track—the dragsters. These colorful, supercharged machines line up on the drag strip. They will soon blast down the track in a furious burst of speed and ear-splitting noise.

Burnout...

The burnout! Great clouds of white smoke lift from the strip as the powerful engines roar to life. With the brake on, the rider guns the engine to "wear in" the rear tire. The smooth tire spins on the hard track, heating up the rubber for the best traction on the takeoff.

…and blast off.

In drag racing, two dragsters at a time nose up to the starting line for a race that lasts only a few seconds. But the speed they reach in those few seconds is unbelievable! Speed is the name of the game on the drag strip.

The "triple" dragster is an attention getter.

"Triple" dragsters race in the "unlimited" class. These strange-looking machines have three engines and extended frames. Like all dragsters, they carry their fuel in a pipe that runs the length of the cycle over the engines. The rider straddles the fuel pipe during the race.

Blurring the scene.

Each drag race starts with a deafening roar, as the powerful cycles blast down the strip. Tires screech, then grab—and the riders push their bikes to the limit. For the fans, the scene is a blur of fast-moving color. For the riders, it is the moment of truth.

A "wheelie" in the background.

It takes a lot of strength and skill to control these big, shaking dragsters. If a rider gives the hand throttle too much of a twist at the start, the front wheel of the heavy bike may lift off the ground. This is called a "wheelie." It makes the rider lose time, and probably the race. It is also very dangerous, because the cycle can flip over backwards.

Running straight and true.

You need skill and steel nerves to be a drag-strip winner. You also need the fastest blast from the starting line, and a straight, true run down the strip with both wheels on the ground. That's what every drag racer wants. And that's what the winners get.

The space age comes to the Salt Flats.

It may look like the landscape on the moon, but it is the Salt Flats on the Great Salt Lake Desert in Utah. This speedway is a flat, sun-baked stretch of deserted land. It is here that many machines try for official world speed records. Street bikes and dragsters race on the Salt Flats. But not one of them can come even close to this motorcycle.

The record-breaking cycle and crew.

Meet the Streamliner. It is one of a kind. It was designed and built by a motorcycle rider. To drive this space-age machine, the rider lies down on his stomach with his head near the front of the cycle. His hands and feet work the controls. The test takes place along a five-mile stretch of hard-packed salt.

Twin-engined, streamlined, and fast!

Rider and crew must wait for the right "conditions" on the Salt Flats. The best racing time is usually at the end of the day. The rider must make a run down and a run back within one hour. The official speed is the average of the two runs. On this day, the Streamliner blasted to over 480 kilometers an hour (300 miles an hour)—the fastest thing on two wheels!